Who am I?

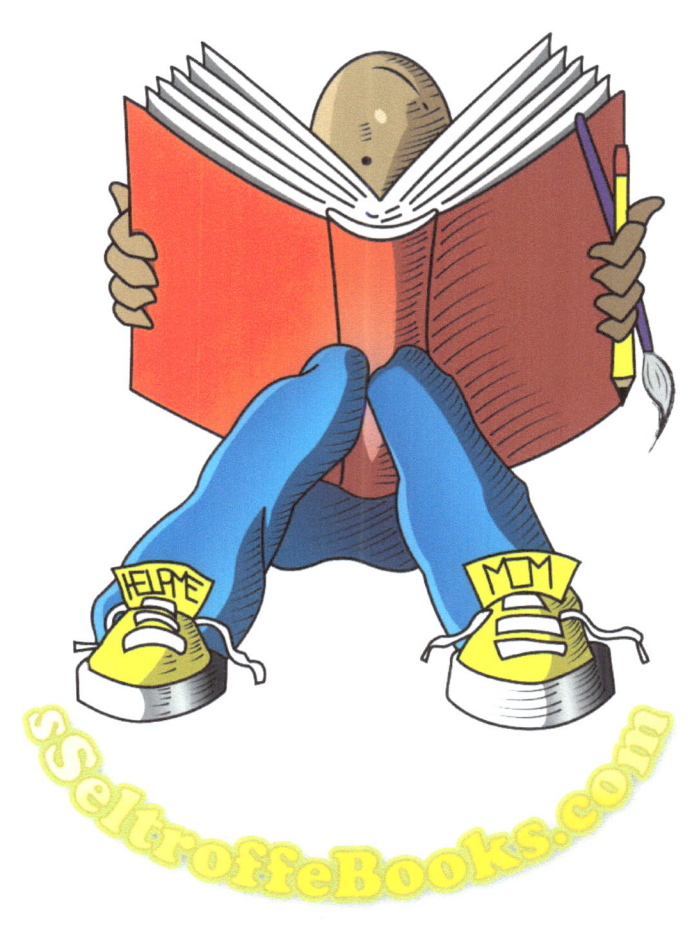

Dr. Raphael A. Mizzell

ORLANDO, FLORIDA

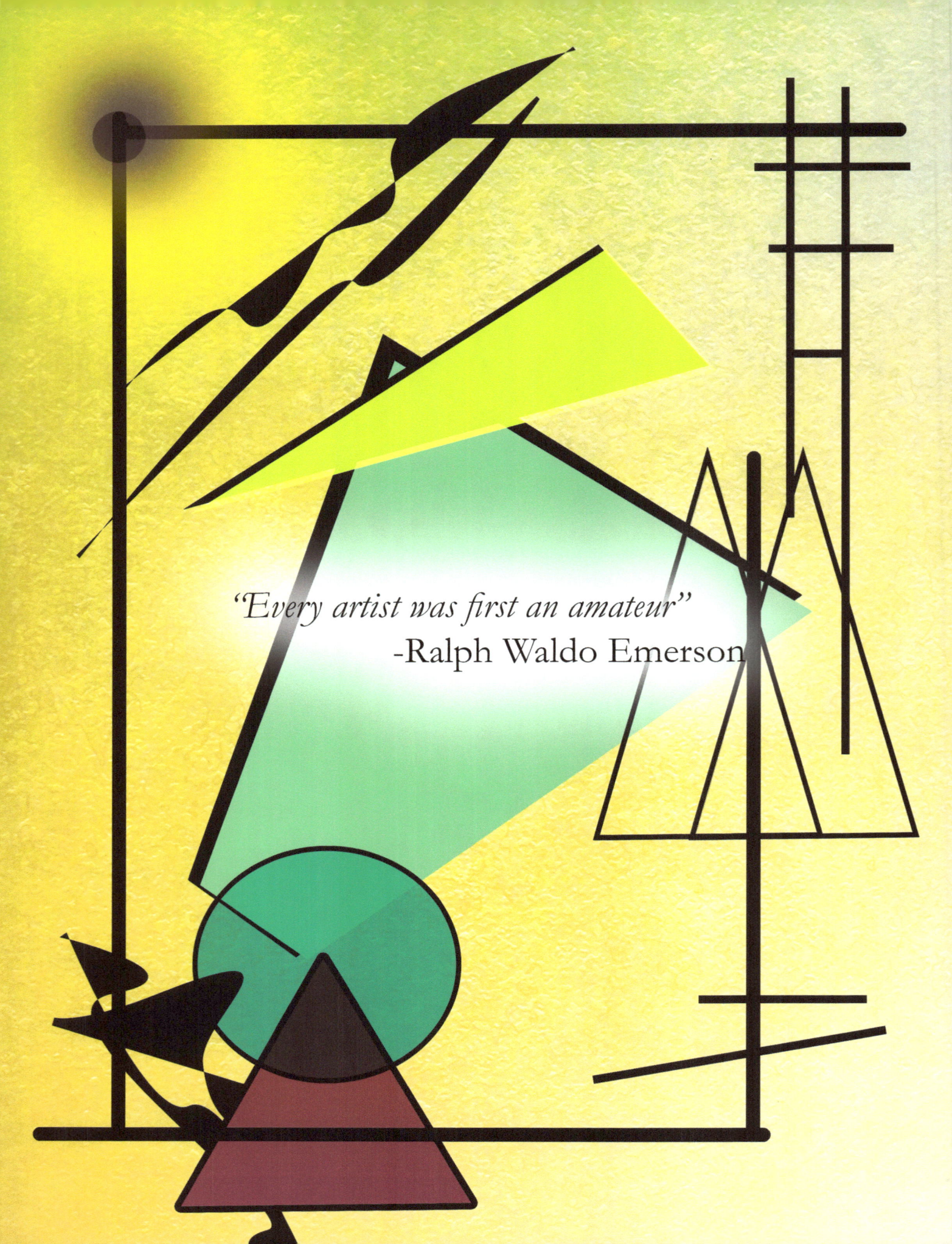

"Every artist was first an amateur"
-Ralph Waldo Emerson

for my mother Betty Quinn R.I.P.

Text and artists illustrations copyright © 2013 by Raphael A. Mizzell

All rights reserved.

Library of Congress Cataloging in Publication Data

Control Number: 2013943895

Text page Illustrations by Tommy Chandler

TommyChand@gmail.com

Graphics Layout by Oscar William

oscarb@trusake.com

Mizzell, Raphael A. Who Am I? Famous Artists

RaphaelMizzell@gmail.com

SUMMARY: This book is about the contributions of 13 notable artists. Artists are listed in chronological order starting from the Renaissance period to Contemporary art, giving you a timeline. The book also gives readers a brief background of the artists, art terms and the characteristics of significant art movements that shaped Art History, as we know it.

ISBN-10: 0976559919

ISBN-13: 978-0-9765599-1-7

*W*ho Am I?

I am an Italian painter, sculptor, architect and a poet who is considered one of the best Italian artists to ever live. My style was distinctive as I created muscular but well-proportioned figures combined with reality in my works of art. One of my most notable art works is the enormous marble statue of *David* which stands over 14 feet tall. My masterpiece painting is the *Sistine Chapel* ceiling; it contains nine different scenes from the Book of Genesis. I was part of the High Renaissance movement, which symbolized "rebirth." Renaissance artists studied <u>Classical Art</u> while incorporating new art developments with scientific knowledge and humanist philosophy.

I am better known as **Michelangelo**.

*<u>Underlined</u> words are listed in the Glossary

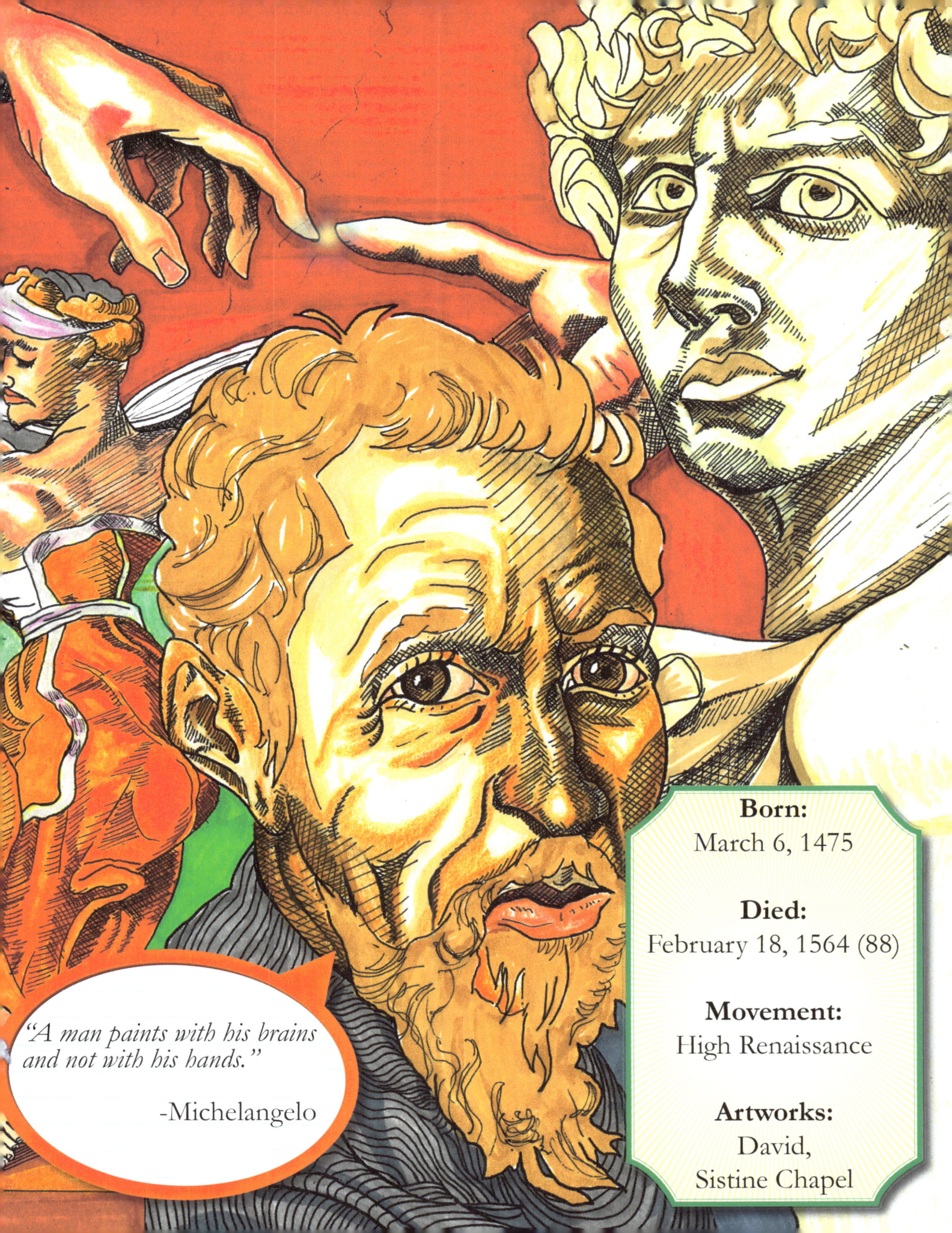

"A man paints with his brains and not with his hands."

-Michelangelo

Born:
March 6, 1475

Died:
February 18, 1564 (88)

Movement:
High Renaissance

Artworks:
David,
Sistine Chapel

Who Am I?

I am an Italian painter who used a style called <u>tenebrism</u>, which was an extreme shift in contrast of light and dark. The Renaissance artist used a similar style called <u>chiaroscuro</u>, but my style gave figures a more dramatic three-dimensional illusion. I was a pioneer of the Baroque movement, which is characterized by great drama, rich, deep color, and intense light and dark shadows. This was in contrast to Renaissance art, which usually showed the moment before an event took place. Baroque artists chose the most dramatic point, the moment when the action occurred.

I am **Michelangelo Merisi da Caravaggio**.

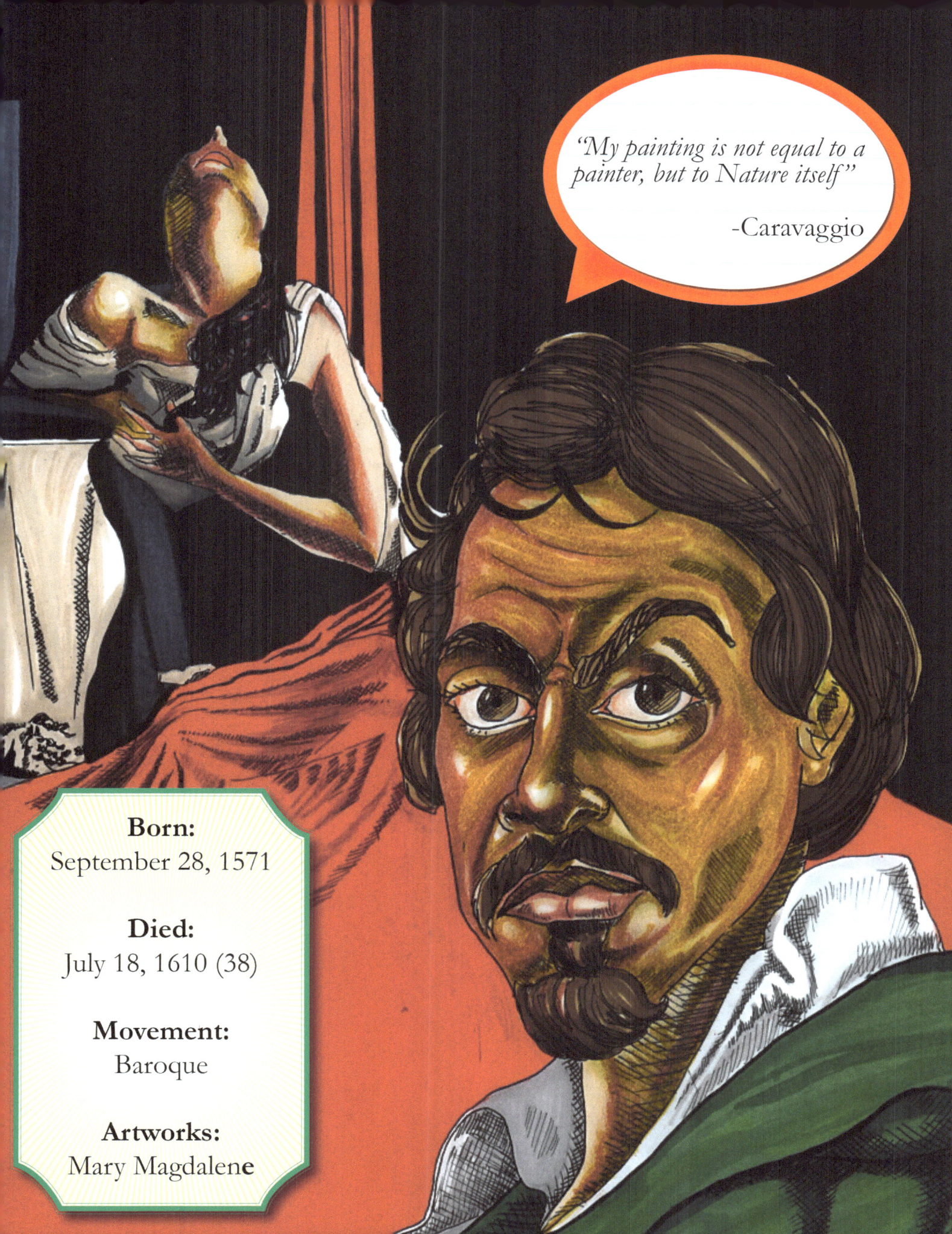

Who Am I?

I am a Spanish born artist and printmaker who was a court painter in the Spanish Crown. I painted numerous royal portraits, paintings that criticized social and political problems. I even painted about the horrors and tragedy of wars. I was a part of the Romanticism period, an artistic, literary and intellectual movement that originated in Europe. The Romanticism period had a strong source of <u>aesthetic</u> experience placing an emphasis on emotions such as fear, horror, terror and awe.

I am **Francisco De Goya**.

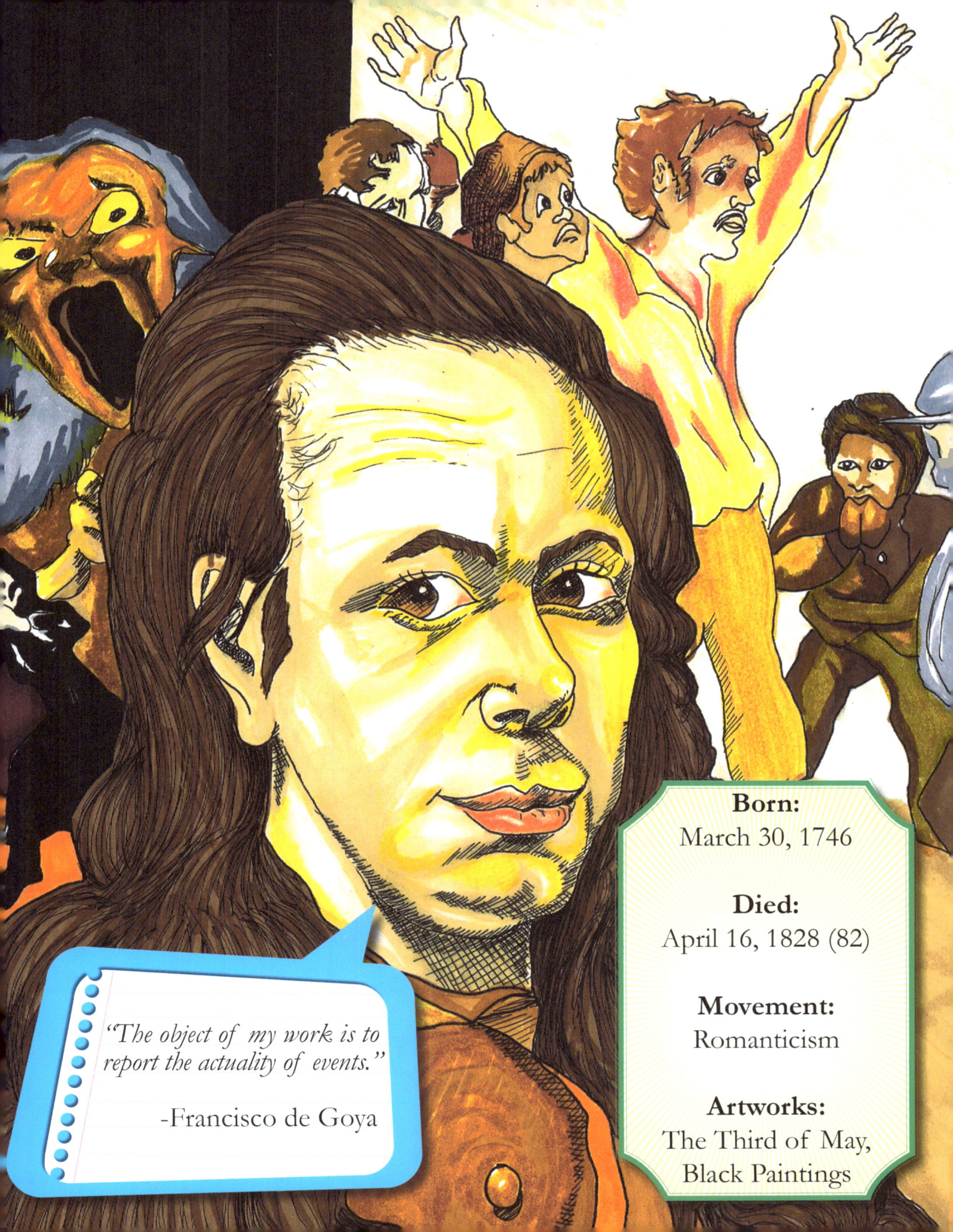

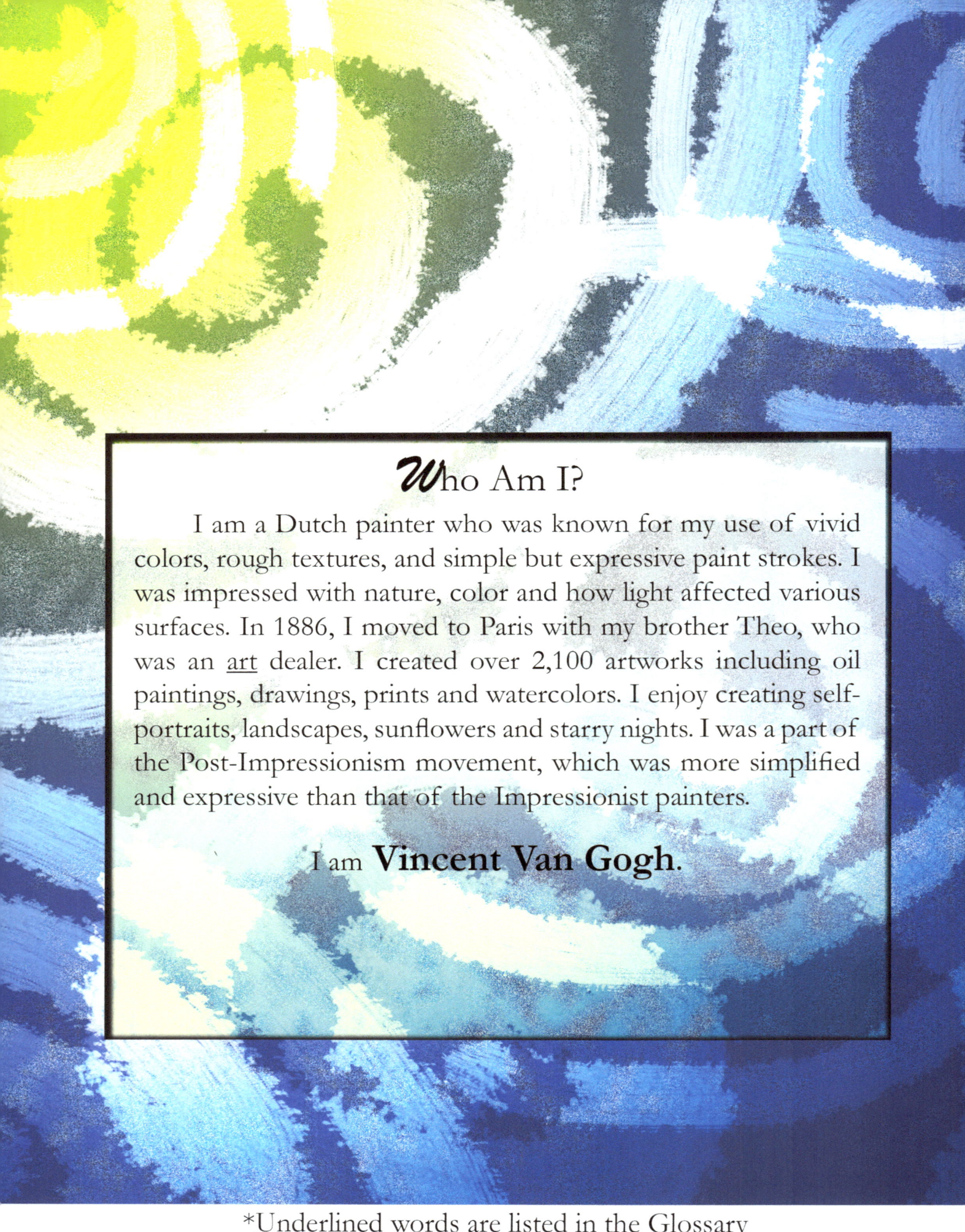

𝒲ho Am I?

I am a Dutch painter who was known for my use of vivid colors, rough textures, and simple but expressive paint strokes. I was impressed with nature, color and how light affected various surfaces. In 1886, I moved to Paris with my brother Theo, who was an <u>art</u> dealer. I created over 2,100 artworks including oil paintings, drawings, prints and watercolors. I enjoy creating self-portraits, landscapes, sunflowers and starry nights. I was a part of the Post-Impressionism movement, which was more simplified and expressive than that of the Impressionist painters.

I am **Vincent Van Gogh**.

*<u>Underlined</u> words are listed in the Glossary

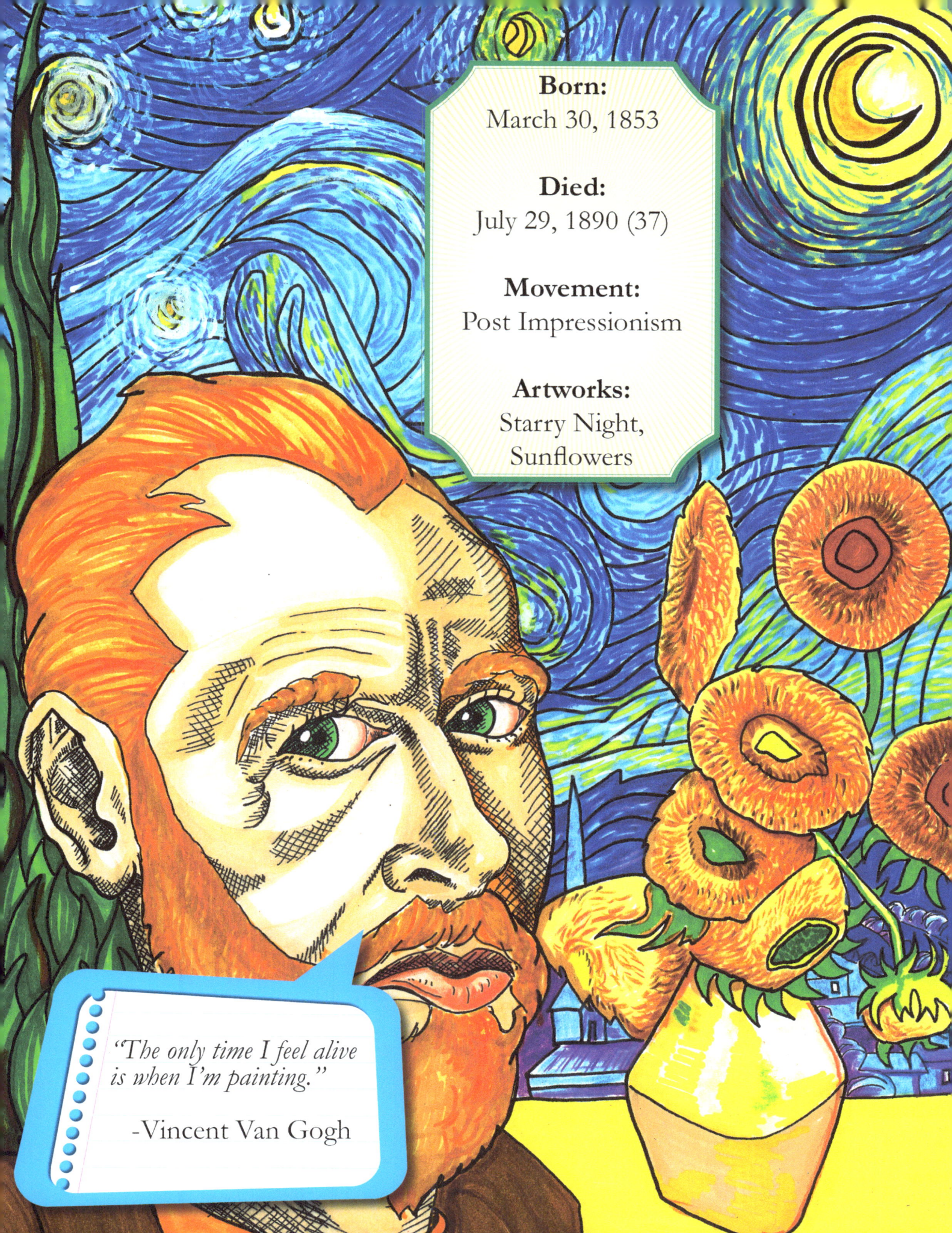

$\mathcal{W}$ho Am I?

I am a Norwegian born painter and printmaker. Early in my artistic career, I studied various art styles such as Naturalism and Impressionism. This led me to create art about my own life, which went deeper and contained more expressive content and intensity. I explored my own emotional and psychological state, which led me to create *The Scream*. I was a part of the German Expressionism movement, which created artwork in a more subjective experience to conjure moods or ideas.

I am **Edvard Munch**.

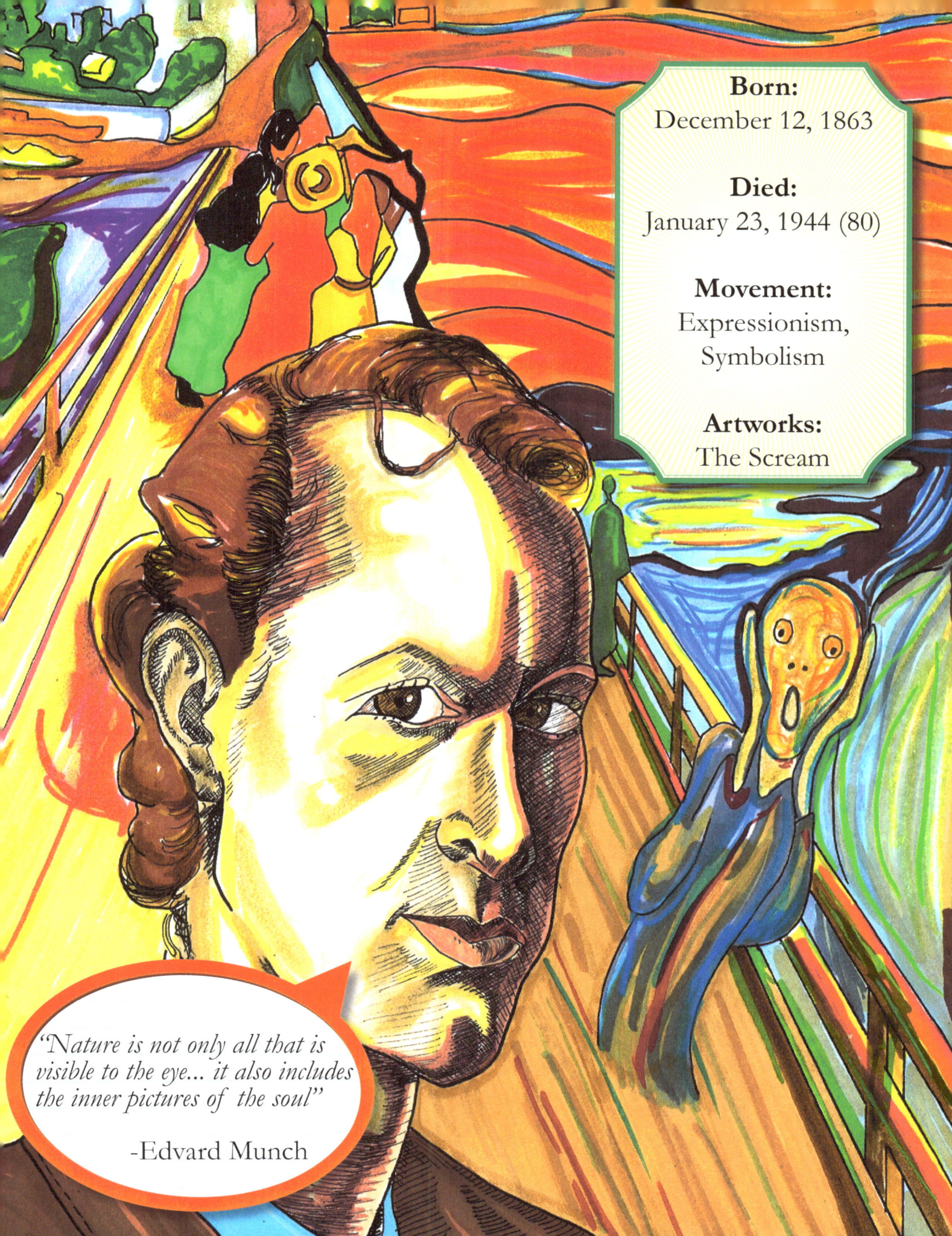

𝒲ho Am I?

I am a Russian painter and theorist who studied law and economics at the University of Moscow, Russia. As an artist, I studied art at the Academy of Fine Arts in Munich, Germany. I also learned how to play the piano and cello as a child. I am noted for painting the first series of original abstract paintings. I was a part of the Abstract movement, which rebelled against the removal from reality in depiction of <u>imagery</u> in art. I wanted to remove all recognizable images in my artwork as my abstract works were about inner beauty, spiritual desire and music. "I applied streaks and blobs of colors onto the canvas with a palette knife and I made them sing with all the intensity I could..."

I am **Wassily Kandinsky**.

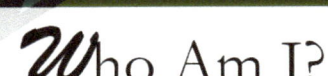

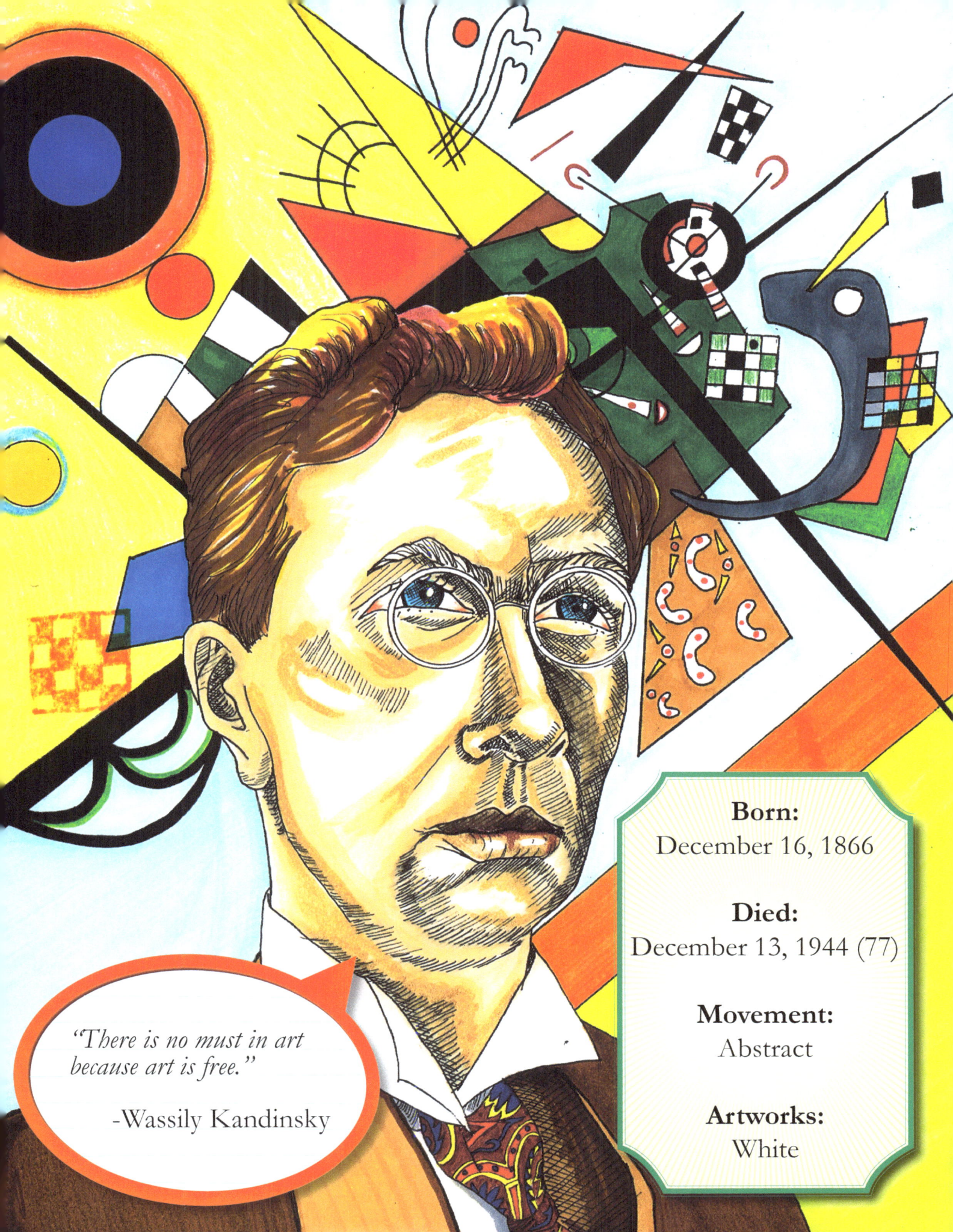

Who Am I?

I am a French artist who was not only a painter, but a draughtsman, printmaker and sculptor. I was known for my use of color, flat shapes and controlled lines in my art works. I was a part of the Fauvism movement; fauve meaning "wild animals" in French. Fauvism used wild, simple, strong and vivid colors that pushed Impressionism to the limits.

I am **Henri Matisse**.

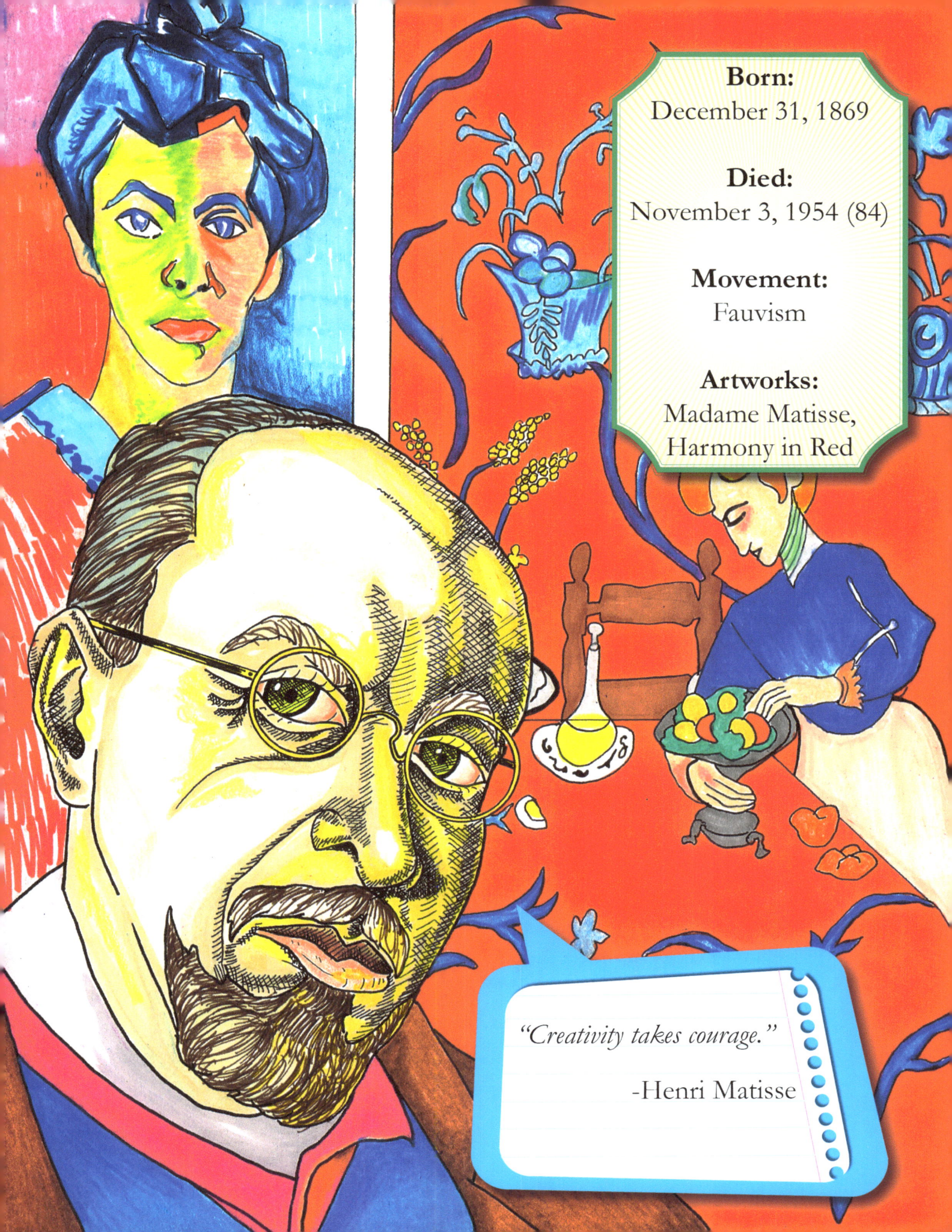

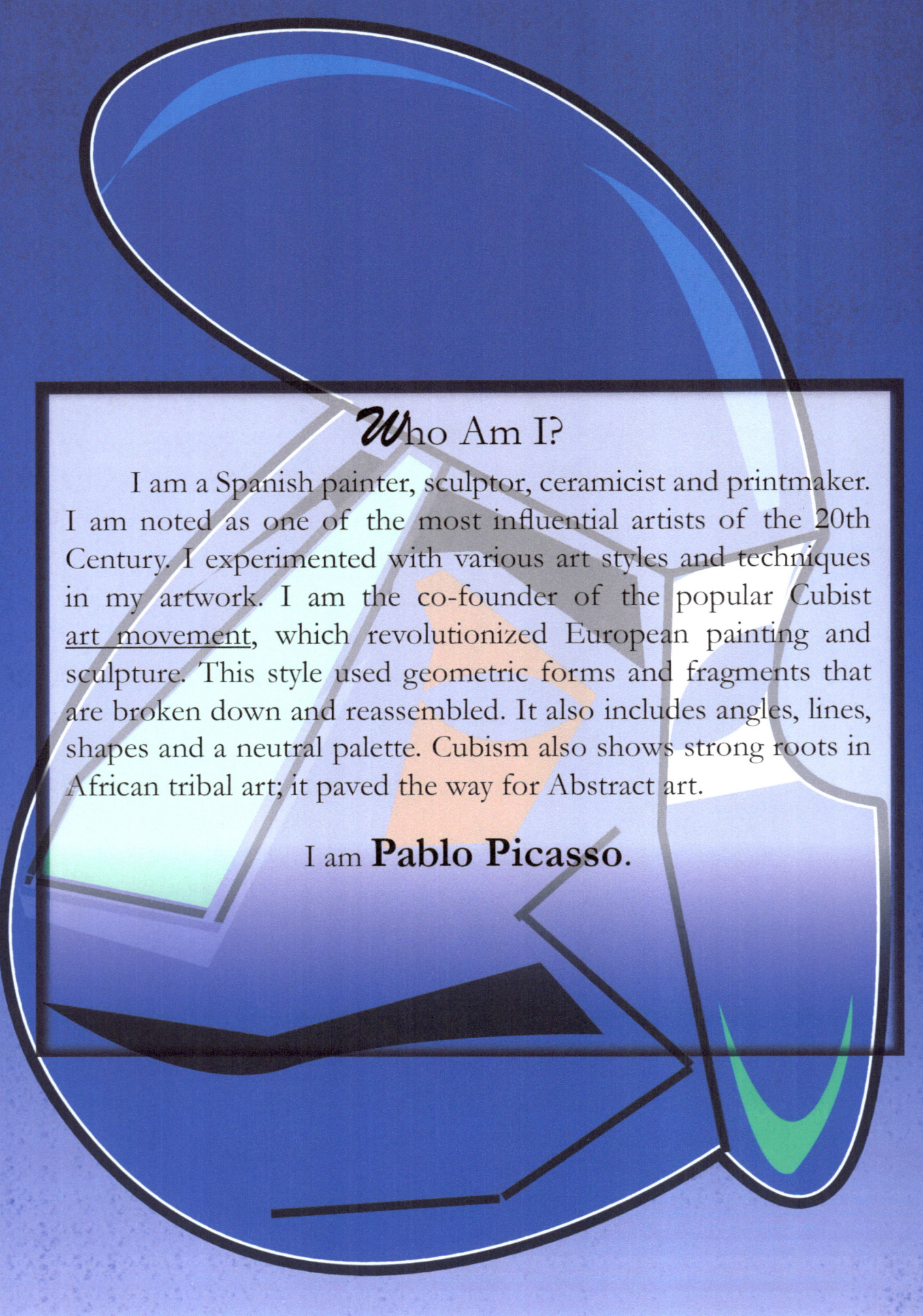

𝒲ho Am I?

I am a Spanish painter, sculptor, ceramicist and printmaker. I am noted as one of the most influential artists of the 20th Century. I experimented with various art styles and techniques in my artwork. I am the co-founder of the popular Cubist <u>art movement</u>, which revolutionized European painting and sculpture. This style used geometric forms and fragments that are broken down and reassembled. It also includes angles, lines, shapes and a neutral palette. Cubism also shows strong roots in African tribal art; it paved the way for Abstract art.

I am **Pablo Picasso**.

*<u>Underlined</u> words are listed in the Glossary

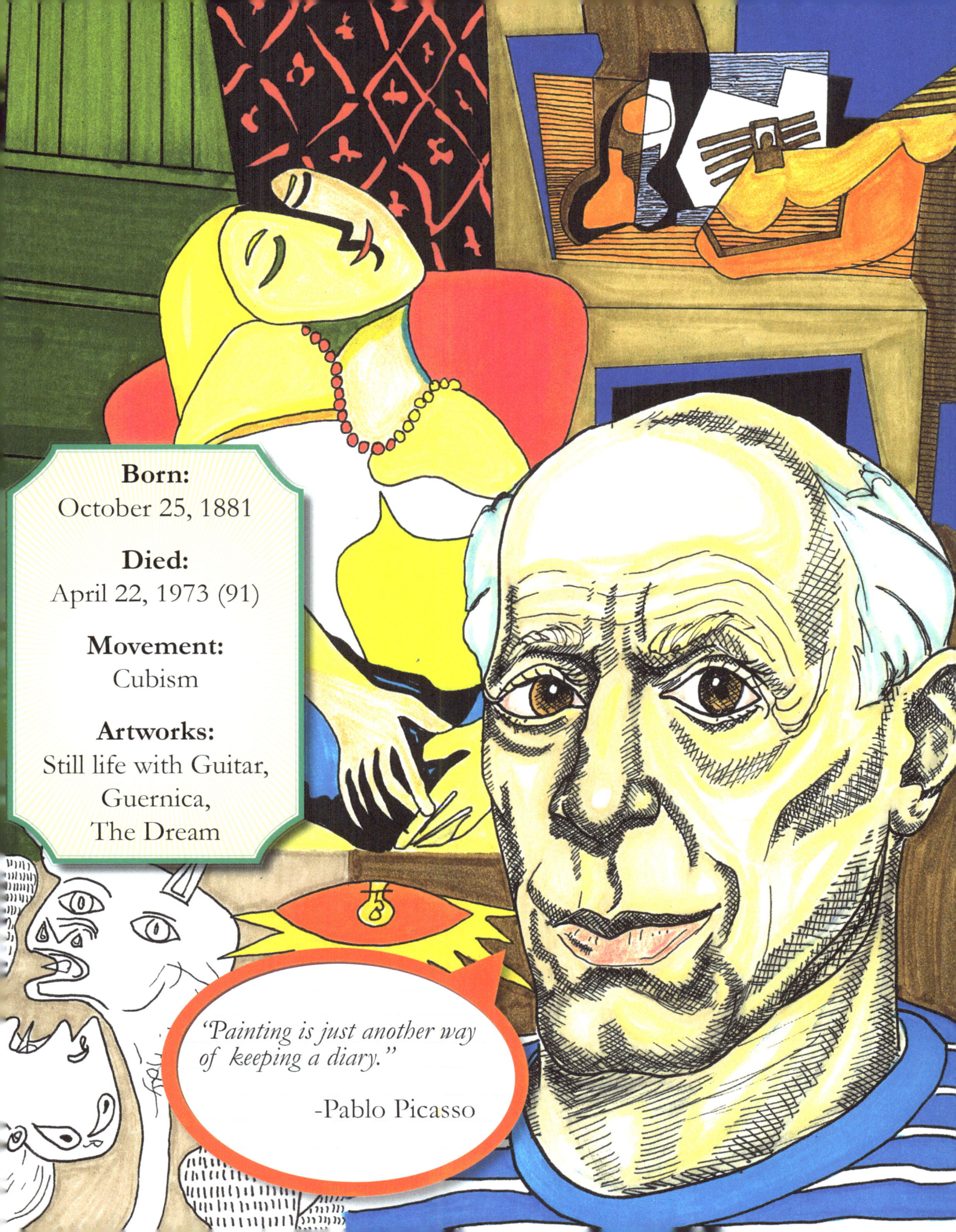

Born:
October 25, 1881

Died:
April 22, 1973 (91)

Movement:
Cubism

Artworks:
Still life with Guitar,
Guernica,
The Dream

"Painting is just another way of keeping a diary."

-Pablo Picasso

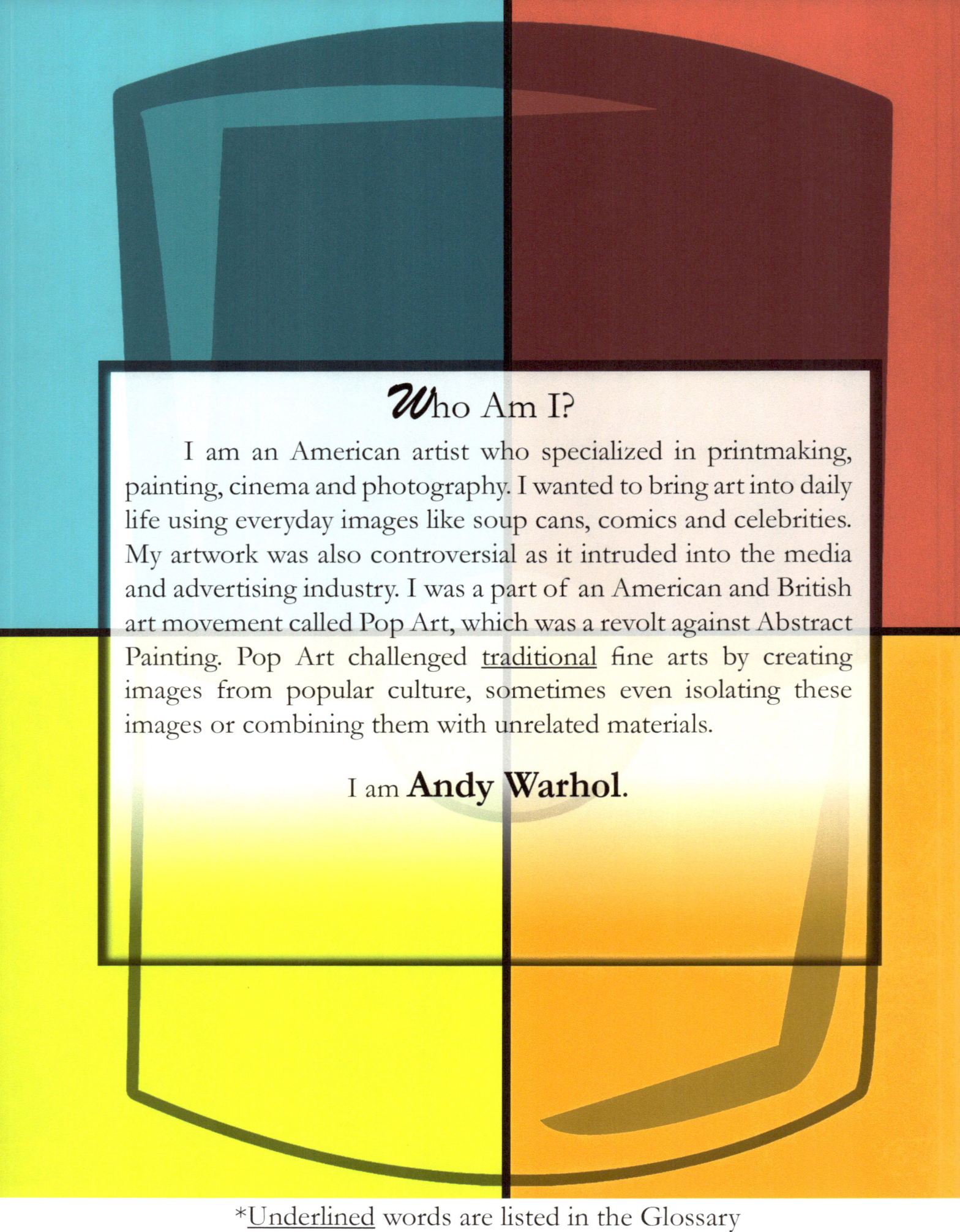

*W*ho Am I?

I am an American artist who specialized in printmaking, painting, cinema and photography. I wanted to bring art into daily life using everyday images like soup cans, comics and celebrities. My artwork was also controversial as it intruded into the media and advertising industry. I was a part of an American and British art movement called Pop Art, which was a revolt against Abstract Painting. Pop Art challenged <u>traditional</u> fine arts by creating images from popular culture, sometimes even isolating these images or combining them with unrelated materials.

I am **Andy Warhol**.

*<u>Underlined</u> words are listed in the Glossary

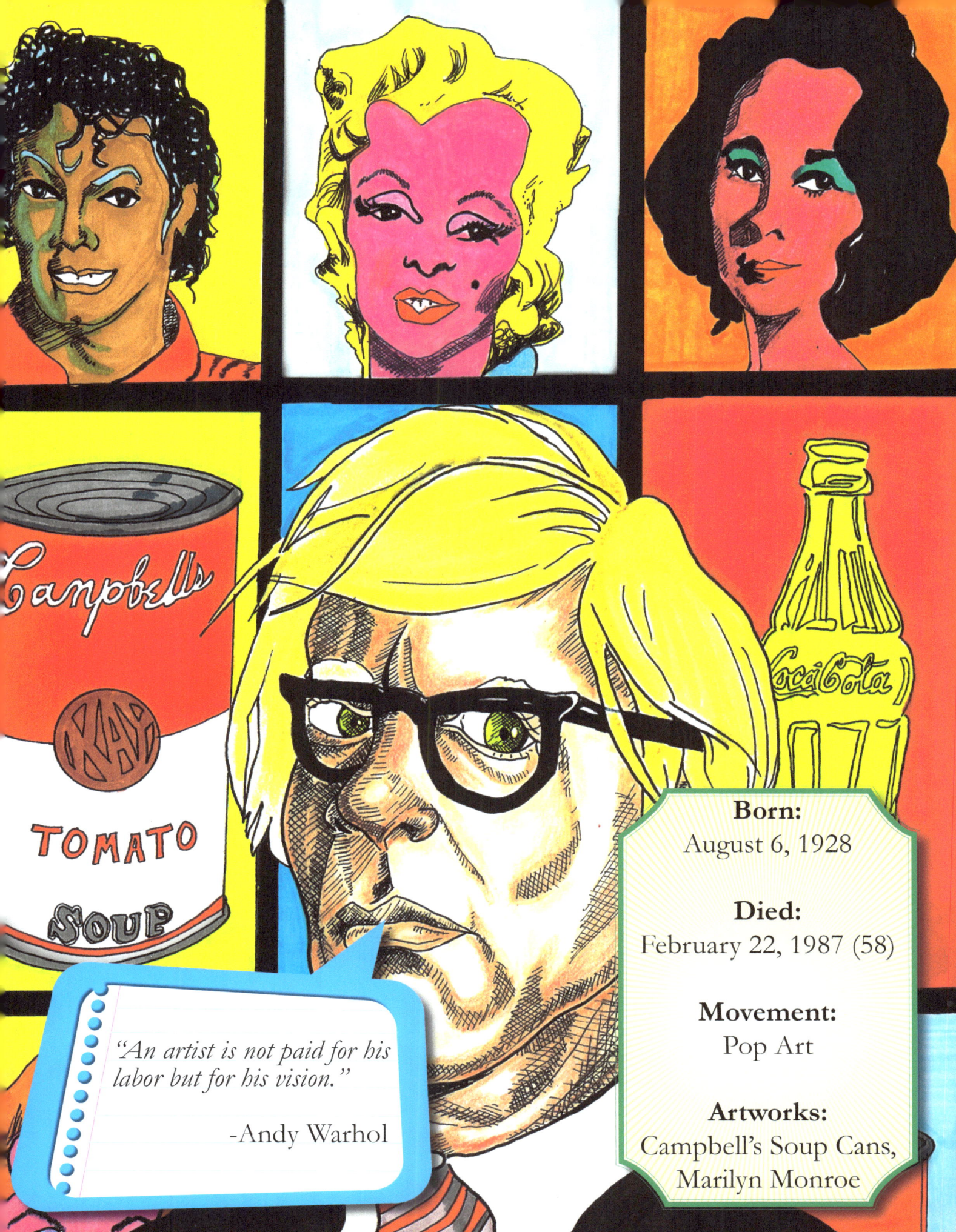

*W*ho Am I?

I was part of an important art movement in the 20th Century known as Surrealism. I liked painting objects that seem out of place, as they are when you are dreaming. I am known for painting melting clocks and disguising faces in my paintings. I was a part of the Surrealist movement, which emphasizes the unconscious and the importance of dreams and the psychological aspect in arts.

I am **Salvador Dali**.

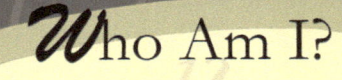

9

3

8

4

7

5

6

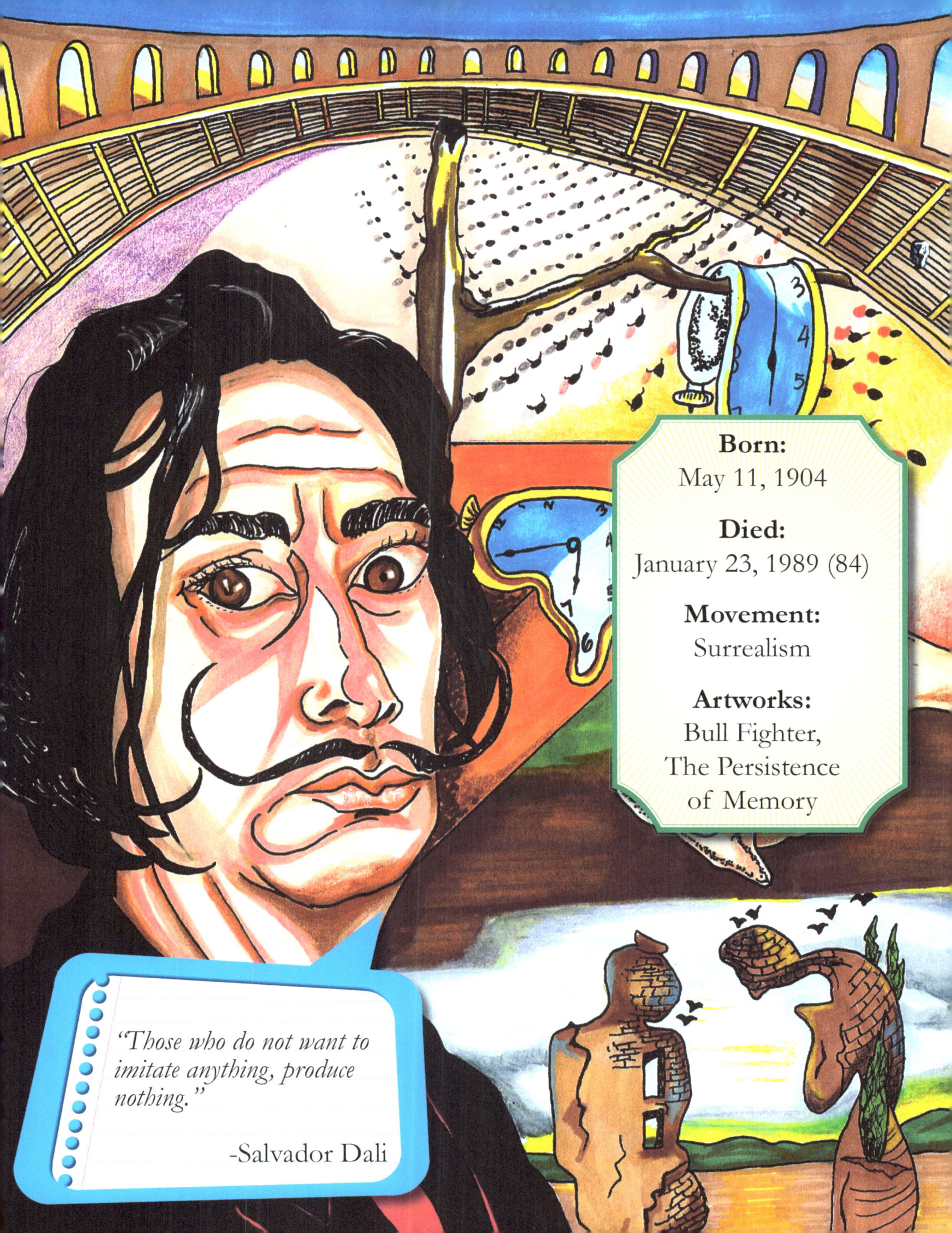

Born:
May 11, 1904

Died:
January 23, 1989 (84)

Movement:
Surrealism

Artworks:
Bull Fighter,
The Persistence
of Memory

"Those who do not want to imitate anything, produce nothing."

-Salvador Dali

*W*ho Am I?

I am an African-American painter and college professor who is noted as one of the most influential African-American artists of the 20th Century. I was known for my narrative series in which I visually depicted a great migration of African-Americans from the rural South to the urban North. I was also a professor at the University of Washington for fifteen years. I was a part of the Dynamic Cubism movement in which I used flame like forms and aggressive resistance of structures. My paintings with movement give off a stillness or somewhat frieze like image.

I am **Jacob Lawrence**.

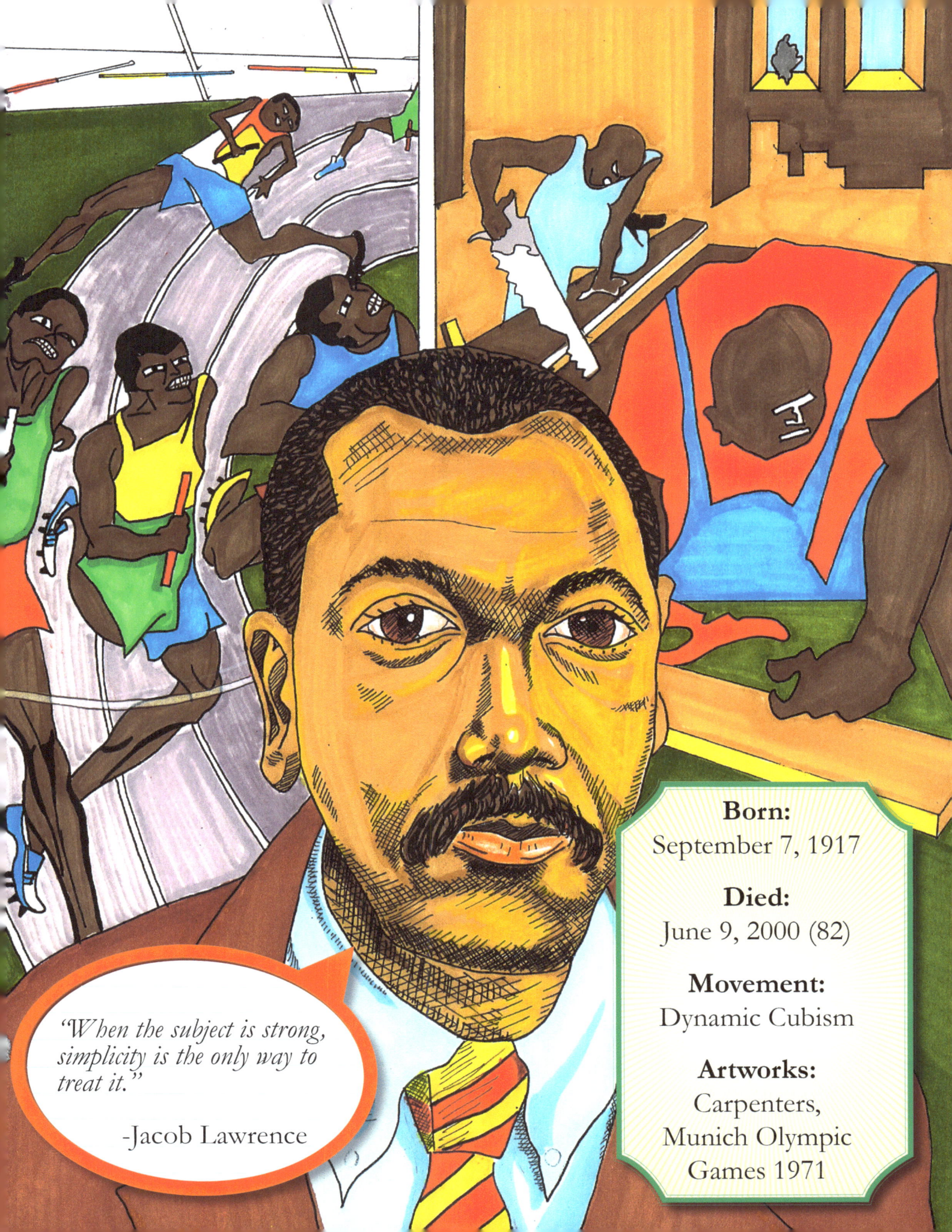

"When the subject is strong, simplicity is the only way to treat it."

-Jacob Lawrence

Born:
September 7, 1917

Died:
June 9, 2000 (82)

Movement:
Dynamic Cubism

Artworks:
Carpenters,
Munich Olympic
Games 1971

*W*ho Am I?

I am an American female painter who studied art at the Art Institute of Chicago and the Art Students League in New York. I knew I wanted to be an artist by the age of 10. My purpose in artworks was to portray the power and emotion of objects of nature. I explored the theme of magnifying flower images in my paintings. In 1985, President Ronald Reagan presented me with the National Medal of Arts for my artistic accomplishments. I was a part of the American Modernism movement that gave human beings the power to create and reshape their environment with the use of scientific knowledge and technology.

I am **Georgia O' Keeffe**.

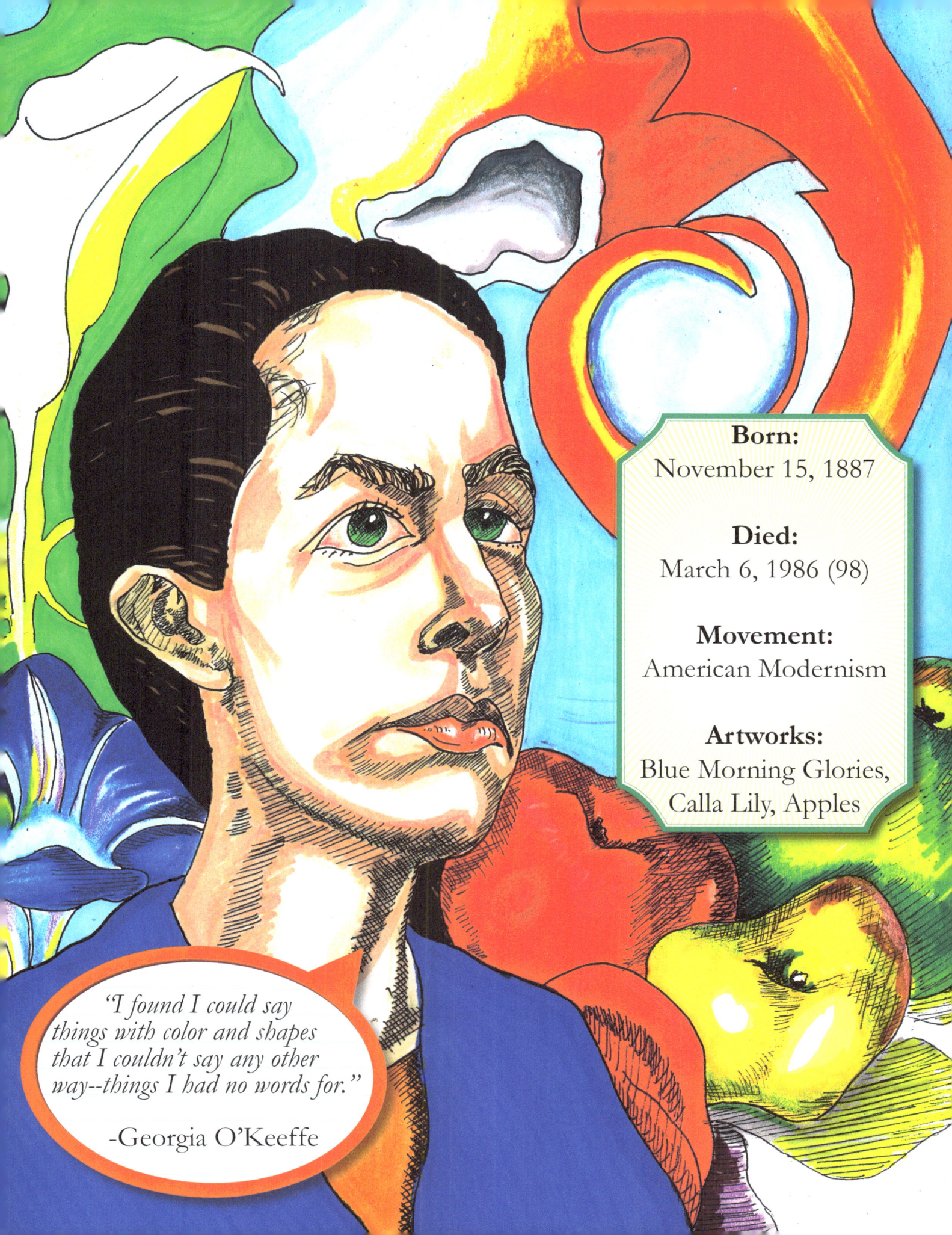

Born:
November 15, 1887

Died:
March 6, 1986 (98)

Movement:
American Modernism

Artworks:
Blue Morning Glories,
Calla Lily, Apples

"I found I could say things with color and shapes that I couldn't say any other way--things I had no words for."

-Georgia O'Keeffe

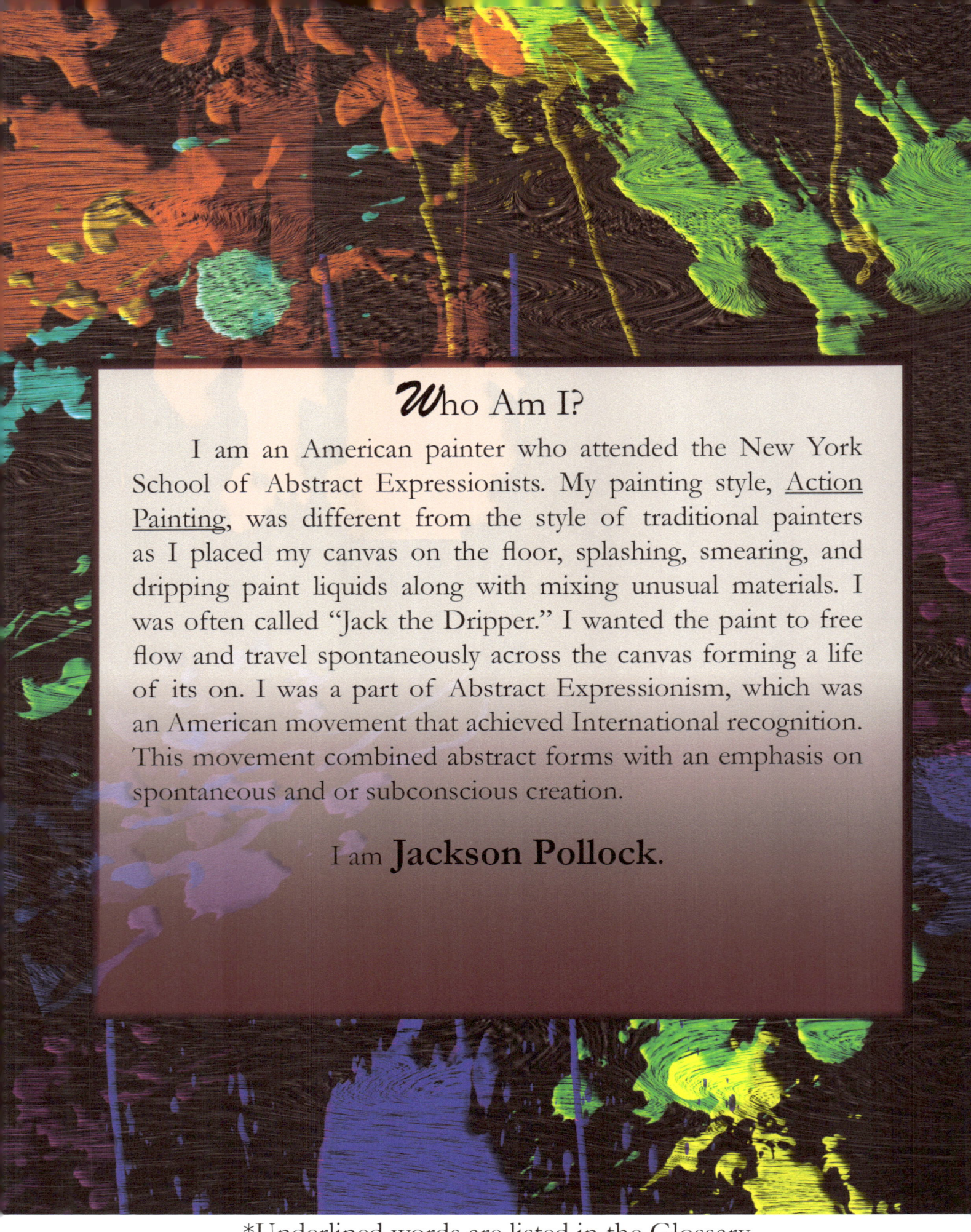

*W*ho Am I?

I am an American painter who attended the New York School of Abstract Expressionists. My painting style, <u>Action Painting</u>, was different from the style of traditional painters as I placed my canvas on the floor, splashing, smearing, and dripping paint liquids along with mixing unusual materials. I was often called "Jack the Dripper." I wanted the paint to free flow and travel spontaneously across the canvas forming a life of its on. I was a part of Abstract Expressionism, which was an American movement that achieved International recognition. This movement combined abstract forms with an emphasis on spontaneous and or subconscious creation.

I am **Jackson Pollock**.

*<u>Underlined</u> words are listed in the Glossary

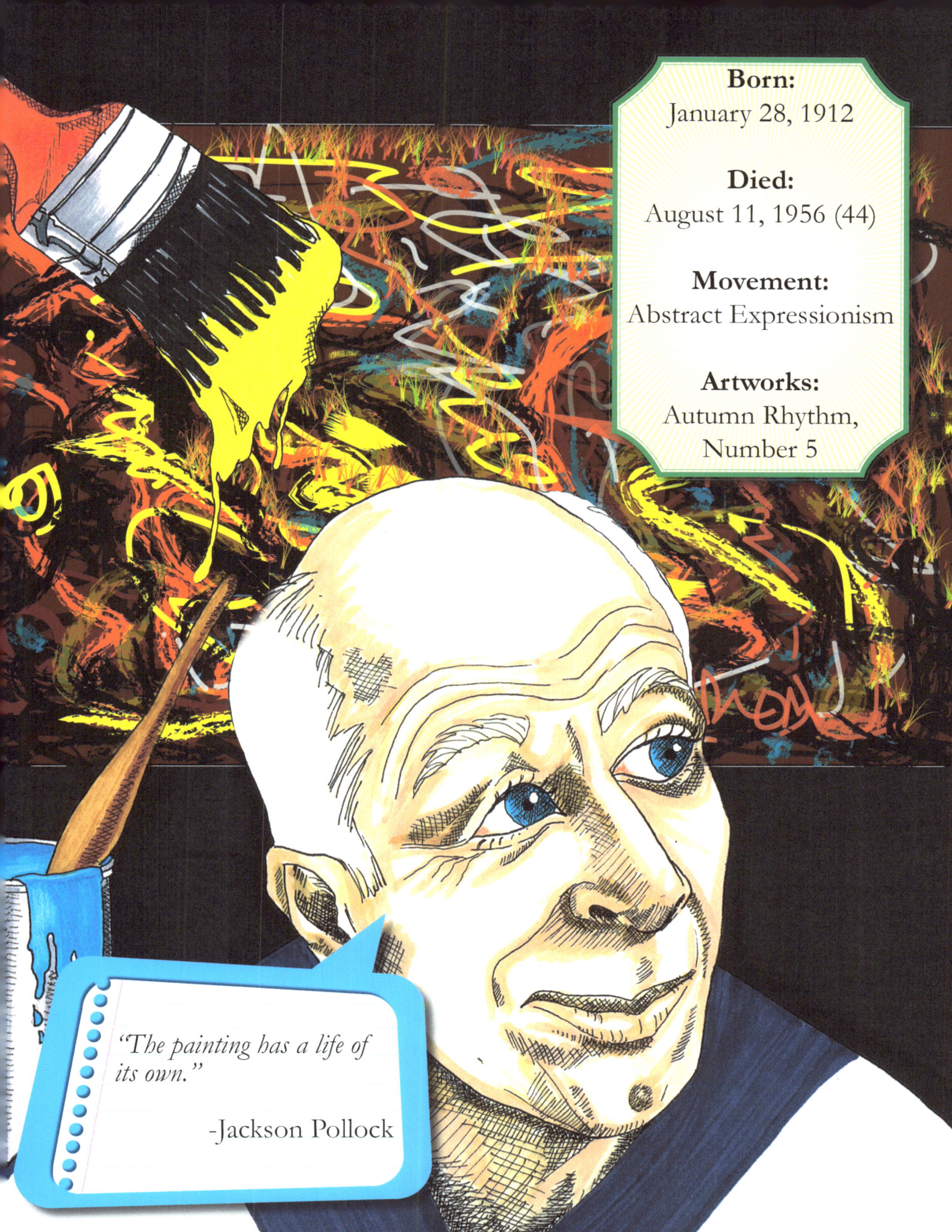

Glossary

Aesthetics is a branch of philosophy dealing with the nature of art, beauty, and taste, with the creation and appreciation of beauty.

Action Painting, sometimes called "gestural abstraction," is a style of painting in which paint is spontaneously dribbled, splashed or smeared onto the canvas, rather than being carefully applied.

Art is a diverse range of human activities and the products of those activities; this context focuses primarily on the visual arts, which includes the creation of images or objects in fields including painting, sculpture, printmaking, photography, and other visual media.

Art movement is a tendency or style in art with a specific common philosophy or goal, followed by a group of artists during a restricted period of time. Art movements were especially important in modern art.

Chiaroscuro in art is the use of strong contrasts between light and dark, usually bold contrasts affecting a whole composition. This term is used throughout the Renaissance artistic period.

Classical Art follows strict artistic principles and rules created by periods of Master Artist Painters, Sculptors and Architects which leads all the way back to the noble Greeks and Romans.

Imagery in art pertains to sight, and allows you to visualize events or places in a work of art.

Tenebrism from the Italian tenebroso (murky), also called dramatic illumination, is a style of painting using very pronounced chiaroscuro, where there are violent contrasts of light and dark and darkness becomes a dominating feature of the image. This term is used throughout the Baroque artistic period.

Tradition (traditional) is a belief or behavior passed down within a group or society with symbolic meaning or special significance with origins in the past.

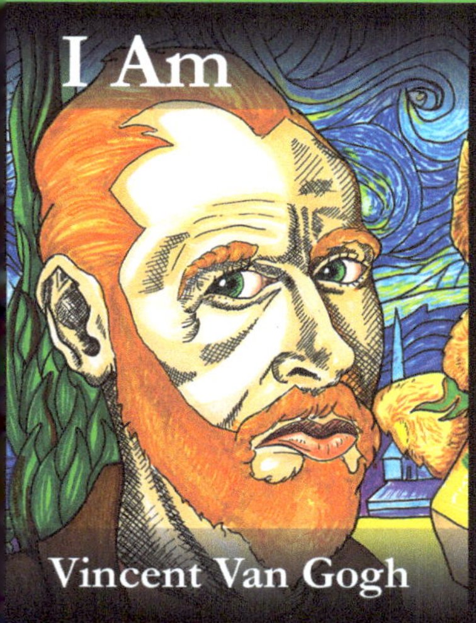

I Am

Vincent Van Gogh

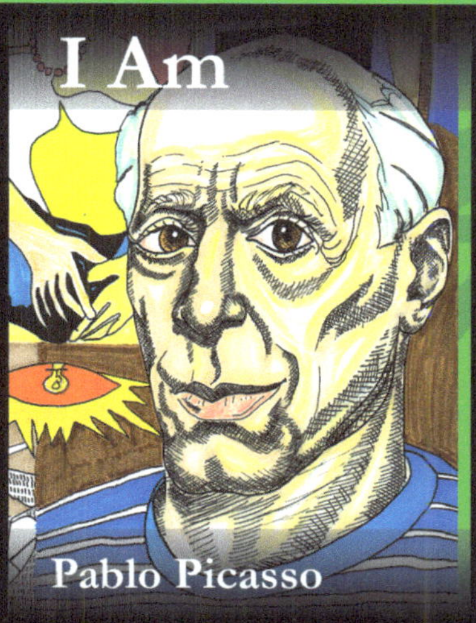

I Am

Pablo Picasso

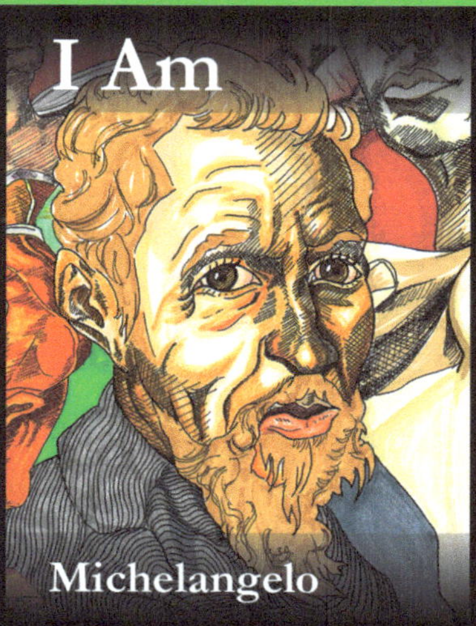

I Am

Michelangelo

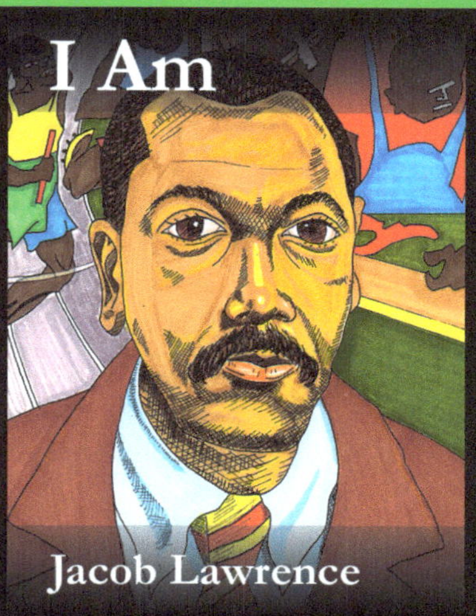

I Am

Jacob Lawrence

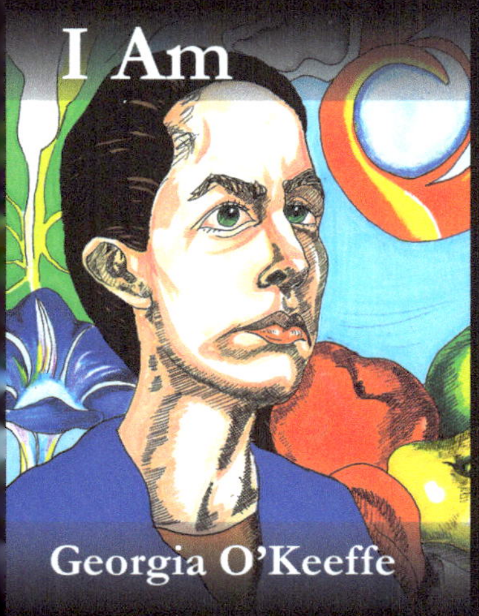

I Am

Georgia O'Keeffe

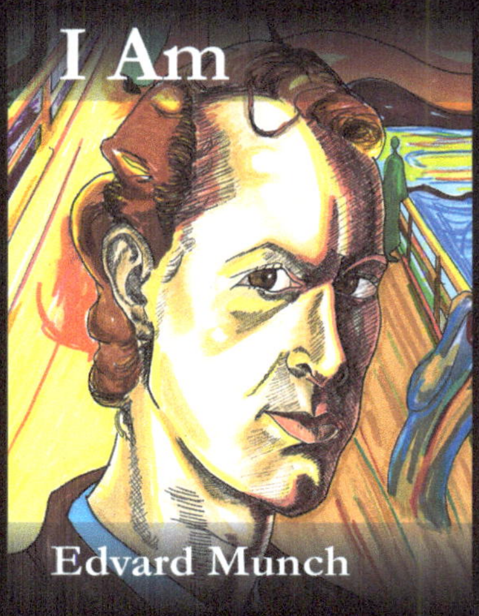

I Am

Edvard Munch

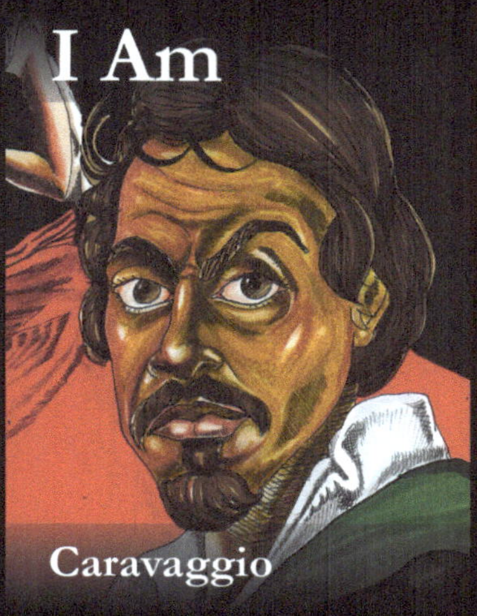

I Am

Caravaggio

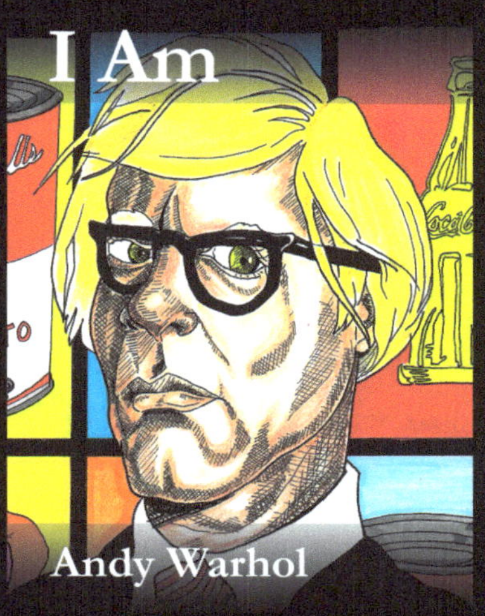

I Am

Andy Warhol

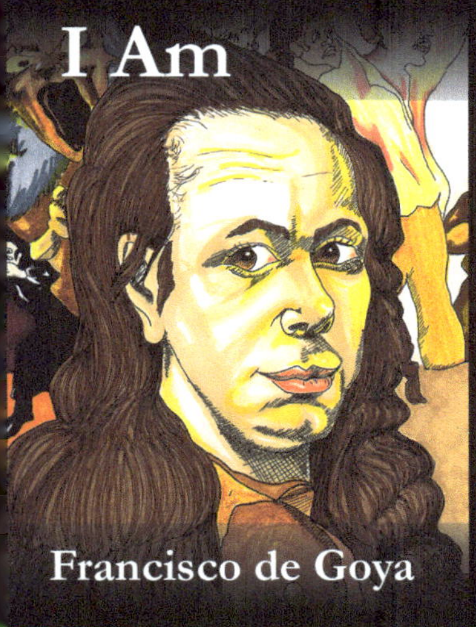

I Am

Francisco de Goya

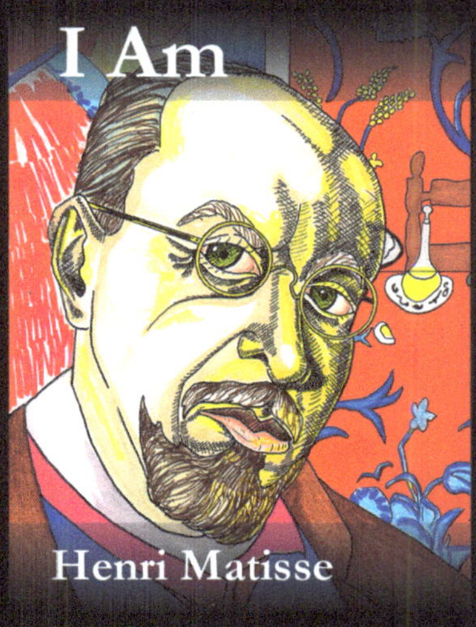

I Am

Henri Matisse

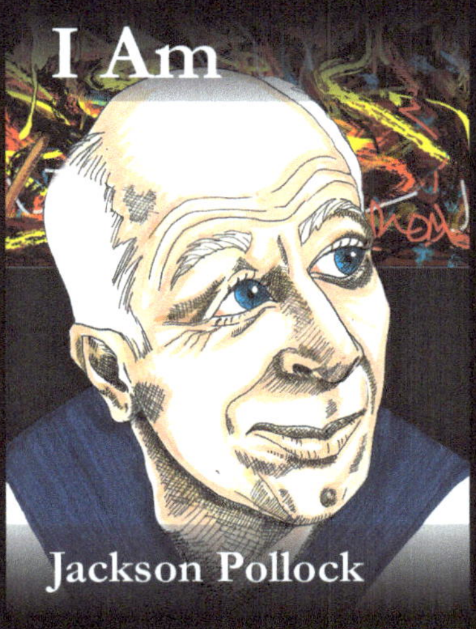

I Am

Jackson Pollock

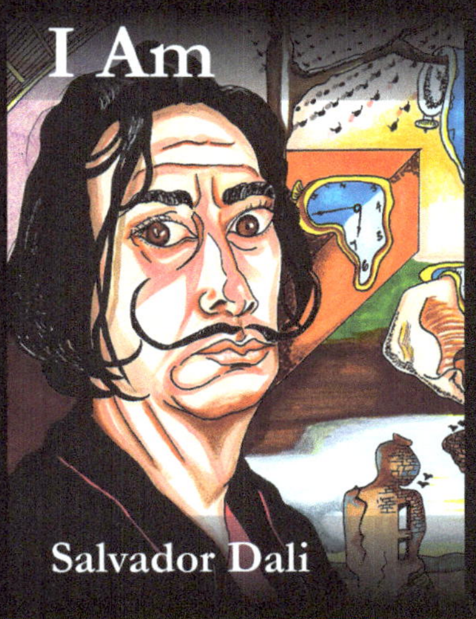

I Am

Salvador Dali

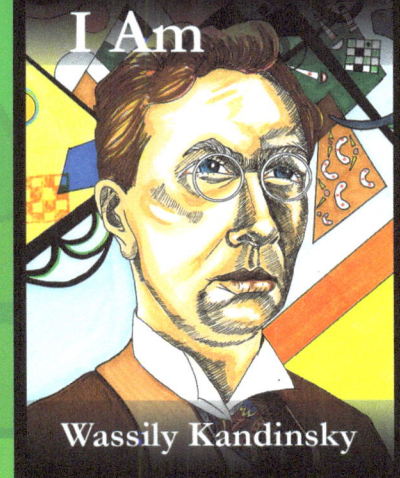

I Am

Wassily Kandinsky

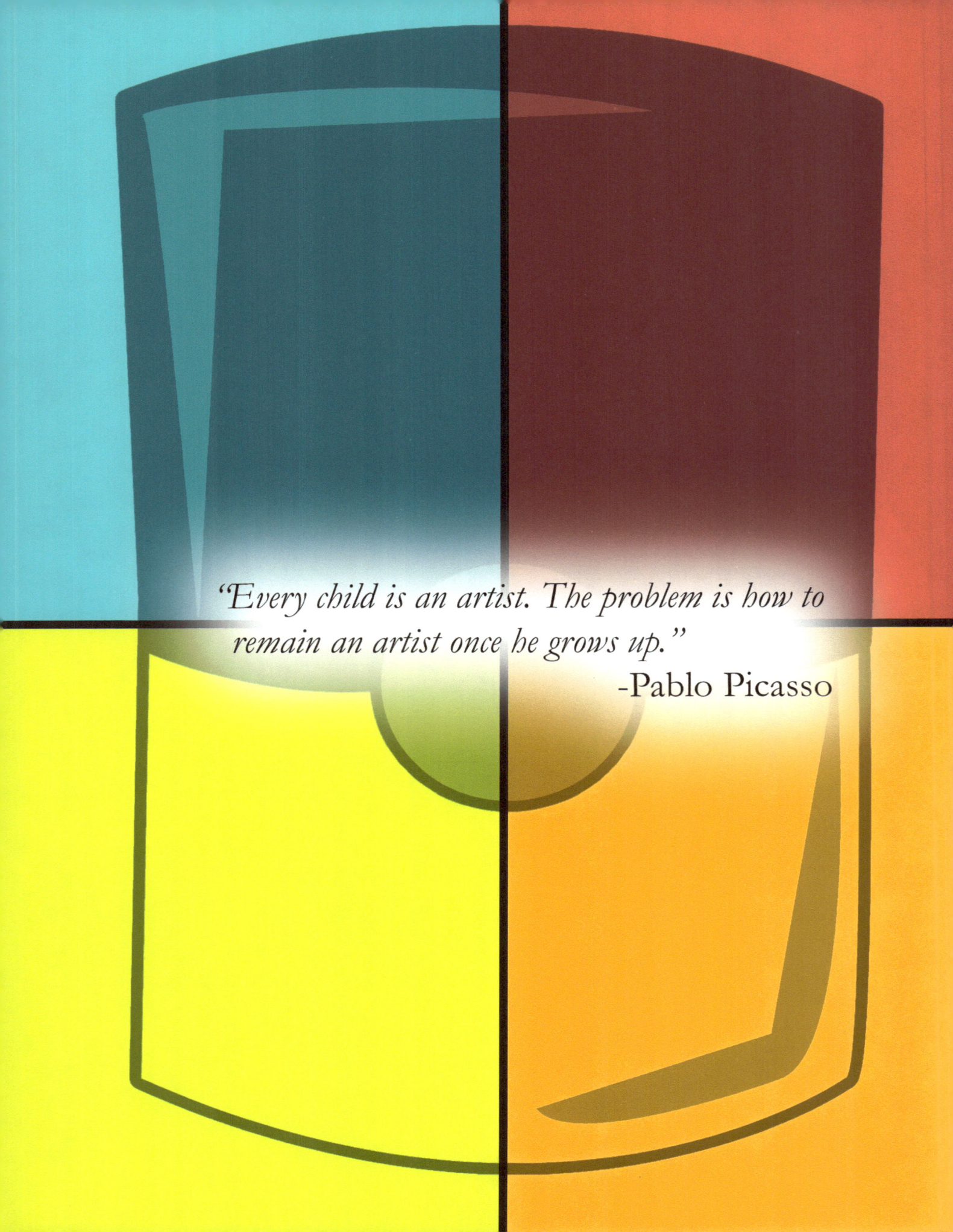

"*Every child is an artist. The problem is how to remain an artist once he grows up.*"

-Pablo Picasso